Usborne

Halloween
things to
make and do

Designed by Kate Rimmer
and Carly Davies

Illustrated by Manola Caprini
and Beatrice Xompero

Words by Kate Nolan

Additional illustration by
Claire Thomas and Krysia Ellis
Digital manipulation by Keith Furnival

Always ask a
grown-up to help
with cutting, or
any other tricky
things.

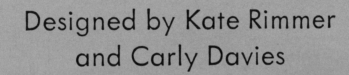

Haunted house

Join the dots in number order, to finish the haunted house.

Can you see five more bats like me?

Finish the monster plant so it matches the one next to it.

It needs 1 eye, 2 sharp teeth and 3 leaves.

Make a ghost

...from a ball of foil and a tissue.

1 Tear a piece of kitchen foil.

2 Glue a long piece of string in the middle like this.

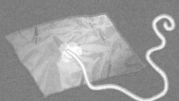

3 Scrunch the foil around the string.

Squeeze into a ball.

4 Use a pencil to make a hole in the middle of a tissue.

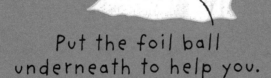

Put the foil ball underneath to help you.

5 Push the end of the string through the hole.

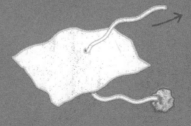

Pull until the ball touches the tissue.

6 Squeeze the tissue around the ball.

7 Add a face.

Felt pen

Make a witch decoration

...to stand on your Halloween party table.

1 Draw around a plate on paper.

2 Cut out the circle.

3 Fold the circle in half. Unfold, then cut along the line.

4 Put glue on one piece like this...

5 ...then bend it around into a cone.

6 Draw around a cup on the other piece.

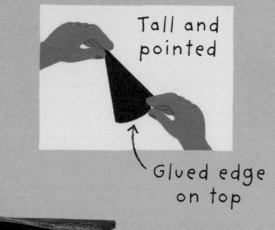

Tall and pointed

Glued edge on top

7 Cut out the circle...

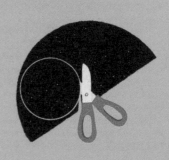

8 ...then fold it in half and half again.

4

You could attach string to hang your witch up.

Add a stripe to the hat.

Stick on strips of paper or tissue paper for hair.

9 Cut off the point like this.

Curved line

10 Unfold and push the circle onto the cone.

Hat

11 Cut a small circle of paper.

Draw on a face.

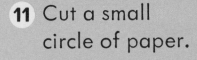

12 Stick it just below the hat.

13 Cut triangles from the leftover paper.

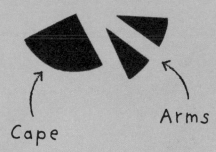

Cape

Arms

14 Glue the cape onto the back of the cone...

15 ...and the arms onto the sides.

Pumpkin patch

Follow the trails to
see who will pick the
biggest pumpkin.

Are there more birds
or mice? Draw around
the answer below.

Spot 3 differences between
these two wheelbarrows.

Can you
find my other
mitten?

Make a paper pumpkin

...using orange and green paper.

1 Use a ruler to tear thick orange paper.

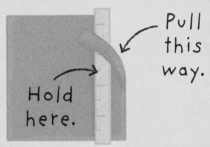

Pull this way.

Hold here.

Ruler

2 Tear four strips.

About as thick as a ruler

3 Stick together to make two crosses.

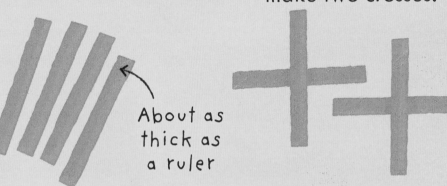

4 Glue the two crosses together.

5 Stick the ends of one strip together.

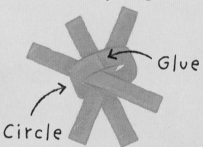

Glue

Circle

6 Repeat with the other strips.

Glue

7 Tear a strip of green paper.

About as thick as one finger

8 Curl with a pencil.

9 Fold one end and stick to the top.

10 Draw on eyes and a mouth.

Felt pen

Werewolf wood

How many werewolves can you count?

How to draw a bat

1 Draw a head and two ears.

2 Add a body...

3 ...and two wings.

4 Draw a face and two legs.

Fill the page with more bats.

This bat is sleeping. →

Spooky spiders

Join the dots in number order, to finish the spider's web.

Can you find seven flies?

Draw a line between each matching pair of spiders.

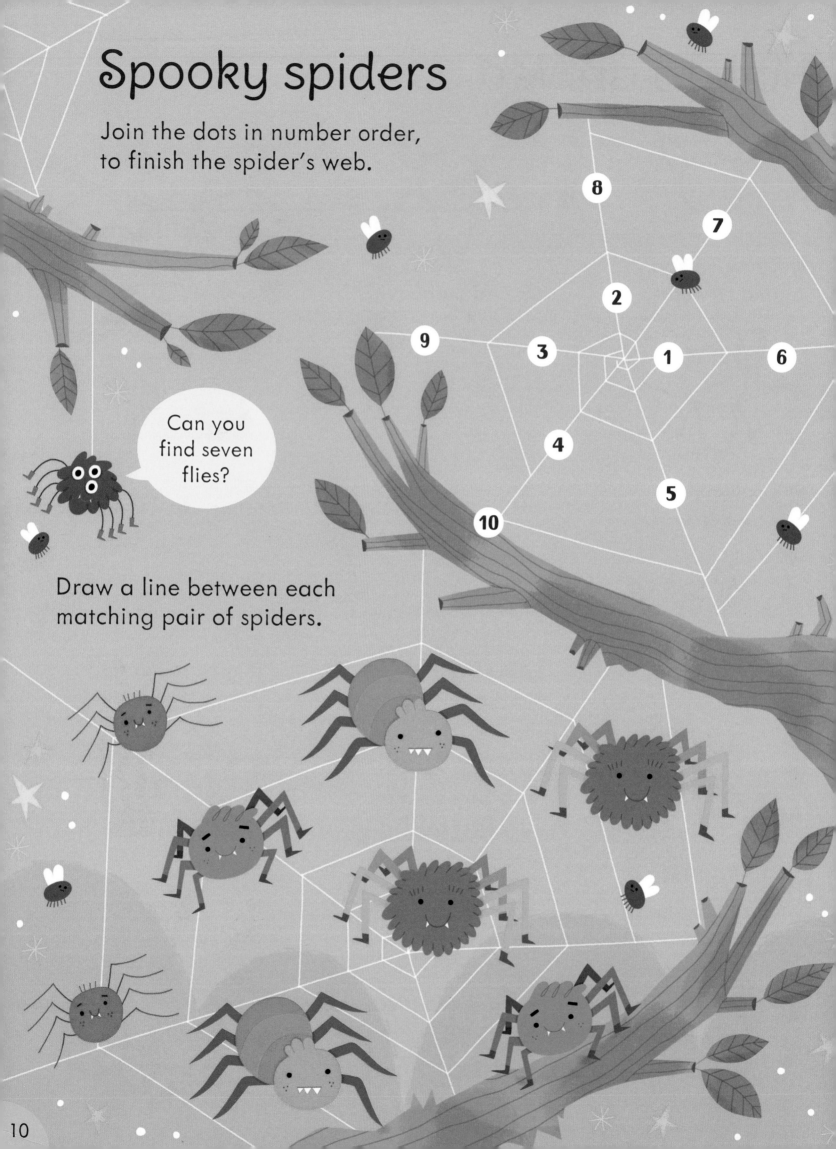

Make a spider

1 Tear one cup off a cardboard egg box.

2 Trim the edges.

3 Cut from the edge to the middle.

4 Paint it and leave to dry.

Body

5 Cut two paper rectangles.

6 Make three long cuts in each one.

Don't cut right to the end.

7 Scrunch, or fold into zigzags.

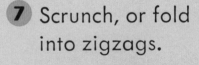

Legs

8 Stick the legs to the body.

Glue inside

9 Add eyes and a mouth.

Make sure the cut is at the back.

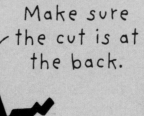

10 Put string into the cut to hang it.

End of string inside

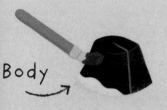

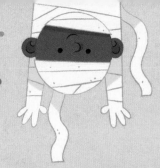

Make a mummy

...out of a cardboard tube and a paper towel.

1 Paint a cardboard tube and leave to dry.

2 Draw two eyes near the top of the tube.

Crayons

3 Roll up a paper towel.

4 Cut into thin pieces.

5 Glue all over the tube, except around the eyes.

6 Wrap your strips around the tube.

Not over eyes

Make bigger or smaller mummies using different-sized tubes.

7 Cut a strip of thick paper a little longer than the tube.

As thick as your finger

8 Stick around the tube to make arms.

Glue at the back

Mummy mix-up

Follow the bandages to see which two mummies are joined together.

Draw lines to finish the bandages on the mummy below.

Can you see my cat?

Are there more flies or maggots? Draw around the answer.

Make a skeleton

...using three paper straws.

If you don't have straws, you could use thin strips of paper instead.

1 Cut three straws into pieces like this.

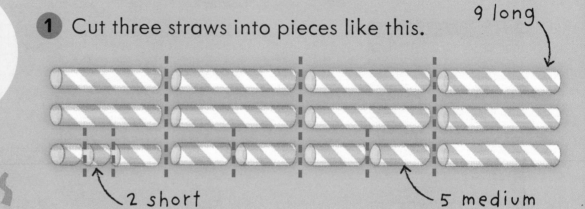

9 long

2 short

5 medium

2 Use a white crayon or pencil to draw an oval and fill it in.

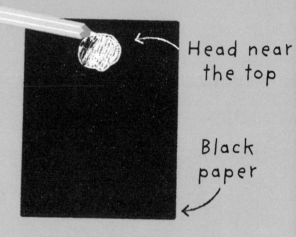

Head near the top

Black paper

3 Glue on three long straws and one medium.

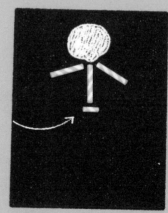

Medium straw here

4 Add two more long pieces to finish the arms...

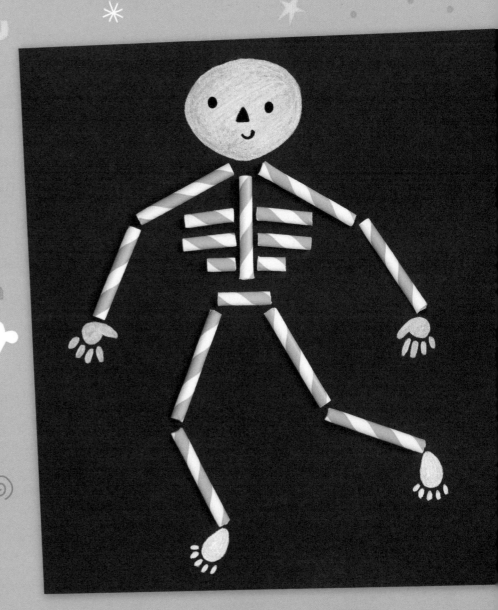

5 ...and four long pieces for the legs.

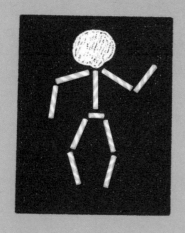

6 Add the other pieces to make the ribs, like this.

Two medium and one short on each side

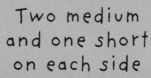

7 Draw on a face, hands and feet.

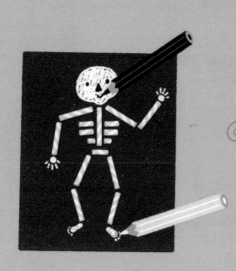

Spooky mansion

Use your pens or crayons to fill in the picture.

Skeleton party

Spot 3 differences between the top two dancing skeletons.

Can you find my missing leg bone?

Draw faces and party hats on the skeletons below.

Are there more red or blue hats? Draw around the answer.

How to draw a spider

1 Draw a body.

2 Add four legs on one side...

3 ...and four legs on the other side.

4 Draw a face.

Draw more spiders on this page.

Make spiderwebs

...to hang around your house.

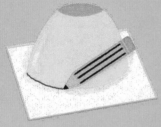

1 Draw around a bowl on thin paper.

2 Cut out the circle.

You could use tissue paper or a paper towel instead.

3 Fold in half...

4 ...and in half again...

5 ...and in half again.

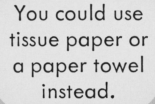 

6 Cut a curve along the rounded edge.

7 Cut out some shapes like this.

8 Unfold your web!

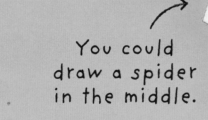

You could draw a spider in the middle.

19

Frightening finger puppets

These paper puppets can become
all kinds of creepy characters!

1 Draw a rectangle
around your fingers
on paper.

2 Cut it out.

3 Fold it over so it
covers your finger.

4 Press the paper down
as you take your
finger out.

5 Glue the edge
of the paper.

Glue
here

6 Fold over and
stick like this.

7 Fold the top over
and glue it down.

8 It should fit on
your finger.

This will
be the
head.

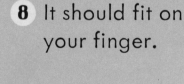

9 Decorate your puppet however you like.

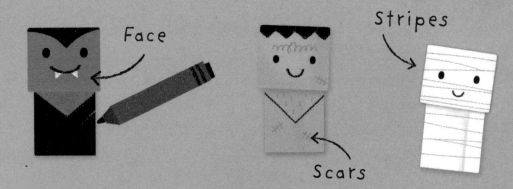

Face

Stripes

Scars

Draw on it with pens or crayons.

Stick on triangles of paper to make a vampire's cape...

...a cat's ears...

...or a witch's hat.

You could make up a spooky story and put on a Halloween puppet show.

Ghost train

Draw a line along the path the train should take to see the most ghosts.

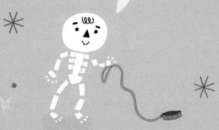

Can you find my dog?

Draw a line between each matching pair of ghosts below.

You could make a group of ghosts, all different shapes.

Make dancing ghosts

1 Cut a shape like this out of a tissue or paper towel.

2 Draw on a face.

Felt pen

3 Put glue on paper and press the bottom edge of your ghost onto it.

No glue here

Small dab

4 Blow up a balloon and tie the end.

Ask a grown-up to help.

5 Rub it up and down on your clothes, hair or carpet.

6 Hold the balloon above your ghost and watch what happens.

Halloween jumble

How many more of each thing can you find?
Count them and write the numbers in the circles.

Can you spot a spider without a web?

Zombie zone

Which zombie matches the dark shape?

Spot 3 differences between these two zombies.

Monster ball

Draw around the monster musician who doesn't look like any other.

Can you finish the monster so it matches its twin below?

I need 3 eyes, 2 teeth and a balloon.

Add funny faces on these dancing monsters.

Paint splat monsters

1 Put some paint in an old bowl.

2 Add a few drops of water and mix.

Quite runny

3 Lay down newspaper and put paper on top.

4 Drip the runny paint onto the paper, near the middle.

5 Using a straw, gently blow the paint.

6 Turn the paper around and blow in different directions.

7 When it's dry, use pens or crayons to add details.

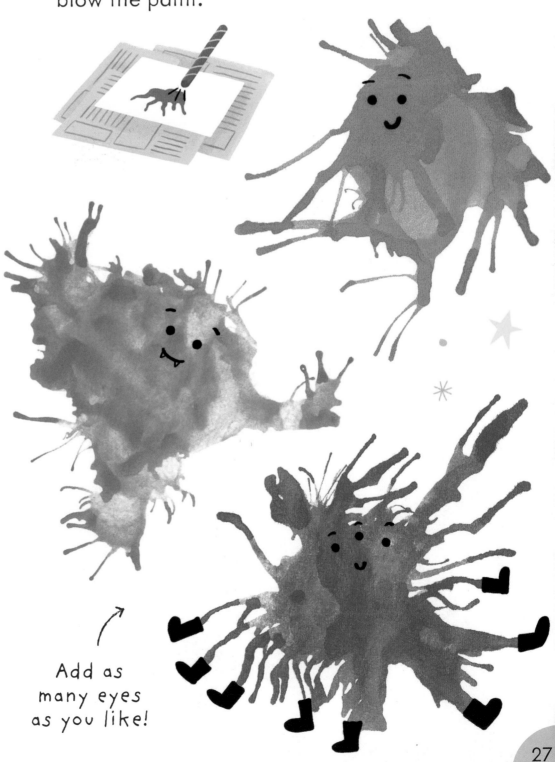

Add as many eyes as you like!

27

Windy days

Draw more leaves falling from the trees.

Look for a bird just like me.

Can you spot two squirrels?

Are there more acorns or pinecones? Draw around the answer.

Draw a line between each matching pair of leaves.

Make an owl

...using fallen leaves you've collected.

1 Find two leaves that look the same and leave to dry.

Paper towel

2 Draw around a cup.

Paper

3 Cut out the circle.

4 Make two small cuts like this.

5 Fold the flap back and stick it down.

6 Draw on eyes.

7 Add a beak.

8 Glue each side.

9 Stick on leaves.

Wings

You could stick on two leaves for each wing.

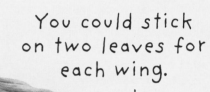

Glue your owl onto paper to make a picture, or add string to hang it up.

Trick-or-treat?

Draw a line along the path to lead the children to the house with the blue roof.

I can see five black cats – can you?

Find 3 differences between these two trick-or-treat buckets.

Make a monster munchbox

This toothy monster is made from an old tissue box.
It's the perfect place to keep your Halloween treats!

1 Tear pieces of tissue paper.

2 Glue them all over the box.

Cover all the gaps.

Fold over edge of the hole.

3 Leave to dry.

Paint the inside of the box if you like.

4 Tear strips of paper.

5 Fold the strips to make zigzags.

6 Stick onto the box like this.

7 Cut out three circles and lots of triangles.

Add black dots for eyes.

White paper

You could stick on different shades of tissue paper.

8 Glue them onto the box.

Stick the teeth inside the hole.

Make a creepy card

...to send to your friends or family.

1 Fold some thick paper in half.

2 Unfold it and lay it on some newspaper.

3 Paint the sole of your foot green.

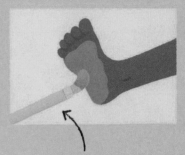

You could ask someone to help.

4 Paint your toes black.

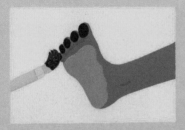

5 Press your foot down on the right-hand side of the paper.

6 Leave to dry, then draw on details.

Neck bolts

Monster maker

Draw around the monster who isn't one of a matching pair.

Connect the dots in number order, to finish the monster's head.

Are there more jars of purple or green slime? Draw around the answer.

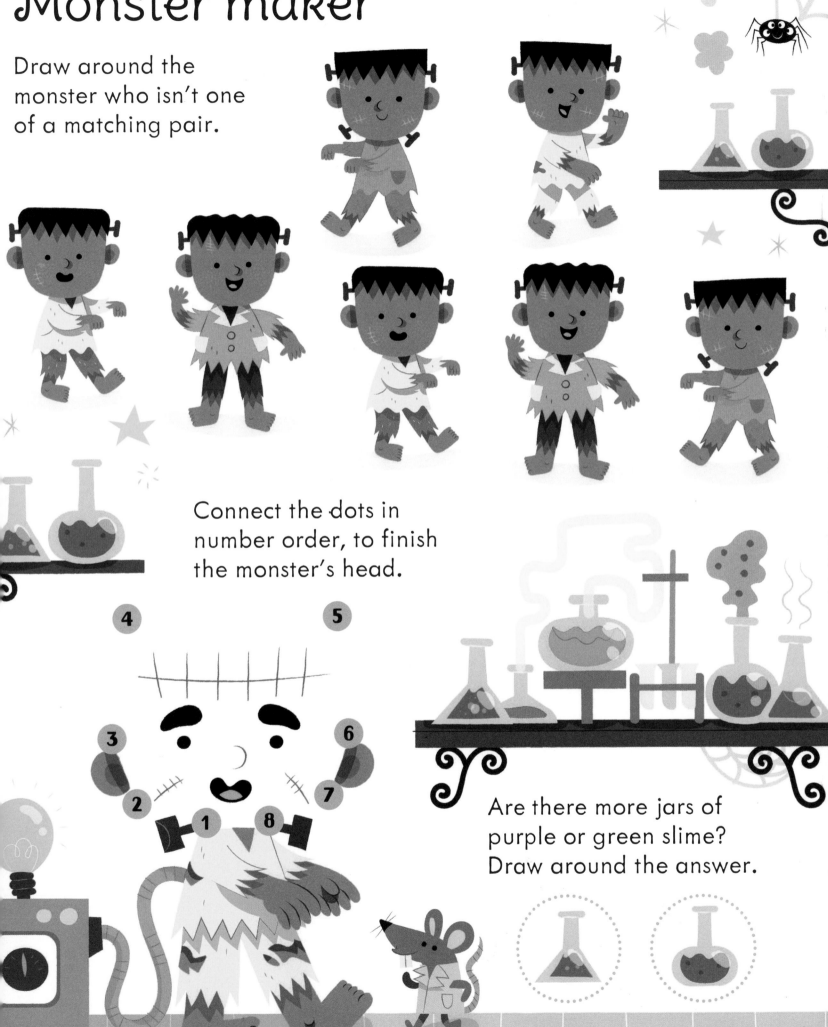

Make a pop-up monster

1 Fold a sheet of thick paper.

2 Open it out and add blobs of paint.

Only on one side →

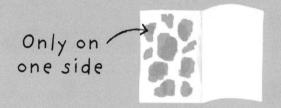

3 Fold it and press down, then open.

← Now the paint is on both sides.

4 Let it dry, then fold it again.

5 Make two cuts in the middle like this.

Fold

About the length of your little finger

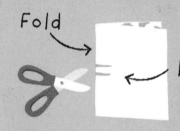

6 Open it up and push the flap inside.

7 Press it down so the fold is inside.

8 Open the paper. The flap will pop up.

9 Cut a monster shape taller than the flap.

10 Add a face and other details.

11 Stick onto the front of the flap.

Slimy swamp

Circle the piece that will finish the picture.

Spot 3 differences between these two swamp creatures.

Can you find two frogs?

Make a bat paper chain

1 Cut a long, thin rectangle of paper.

2 Fold it in half like this...

Short ends together

3 ...and then in half again.

4 Draw straight lines like this on the top edge...

Open end

5 ...then draw three curved lines like this.

Lines don't touch.

6 Cut out the shape along the lines.

Don't cut here...

...or here.

7 Open up the bats.

8 Add faces.

9 To make a long paper chain, repeat the steps and glue together.

Glue here and here.

Make a pumpkin decoration

1 Cut a piece of baking or tracing paper to use as a base.

2 Tear orange tissue paper into small pieces.

3 Stick the pieces of tissue paper all over the base.

Pieces can overlap.

4 When it's dry, fold it in half.

5 Draw a rounded shape like this...

Folded edge

6 ...and cut it out.

7 Unfold.

8 Draw on a face with a black pen.

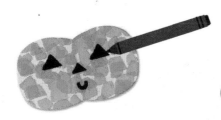

Tape your pumpkin in a window so the light shines through.

9 Add a strip of green paper for a stalk.

Party time

Spot 3 differences between these two party guests.

Can you find six apples?

I've lost my tail! Where is it?

Circle the pumpkin lantern that isn't one of a matching pair.

Make a spider hat

...to wear to a Halloween party.

1 Cut a strip of thick black paper that fits around your head.

Long enough to overlap

2 Draw on six eyes with black and white crayons.

3 Cut a slit going down near one end...

4 ...and a slit going up near the other end.

5 Bend it around and slot the slits together.

Glue to secure.

6 Tear eight strips of paper.

Not too wide

7 Fold them to make zigzags...

8 ...then stick them onto the hat.

See how to tear paper strips on page 7.

Four on each side

How to draw a witch

1

Draw a head and a body.

2

Add legs...

3

...and arms.

4

Draw a pointed hat.

5

Add a face and hair.

You could add a broomstick for a flying witch.

Draw more witches on this page.

Hubble, bubble...

Spot 3 differences between these two witches.

Can you see three more toads like me?

④ ⑤ ⑥ ⑦

Join the dots in number order, to finish the witch's hat.

① ② ③ ⑧ ⑨ ⑩

What would you put in a magic potion? Draw it in the cauldron.

Wizard's workshop

Can you find and circle these parts of the picture?

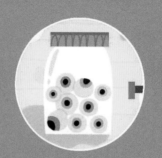

Where's my magic wand?

Fill the jars with more bugs and eyeballs.

Make a magic potion

Ingredients

Clear vinegar
Dishwashing liquid
Bicarbonate of soda
(baking soda)

1 Put an empty jar or small bottle on a tray.

2 Half-fill it with clear vinegar.

3 Stir in a teaspoon of dishwashing liquid.

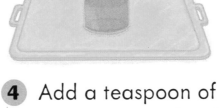

Add another teaspoon if you're using a bigger jar.

4 Add a teaspoon of bicarbonate of soda (baking soda).

Watch what happens after step 4!

The shade of your potion depends on the dishwashing liquid you use.

Warning: don't drink this potion!

43

Full moon

Spot 3 differences between these two bats.

Can you count five more bugs like me?

Find the words below in the grid and draw around them.

bat

owl

cat

d	n	e	o	w	l
x	b	o	p	y	e
g	s	q	r	n	h
z	r	t	v	i	c
u	b	a	t	m	a
f	s	k	w	j	t

How to draw a cat

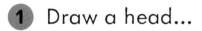

1 Draw a head...

2 ...and a body.

3 Add four legs and a tail...

4 ...two ears and a face.

Draw more cats on this page.

Ghostly gallery

Fill in all the shapes that have orange dots. What do you see?

Draw your own spooky
pictures in these frames.

Answers

2

6

8

8 werewolves

10

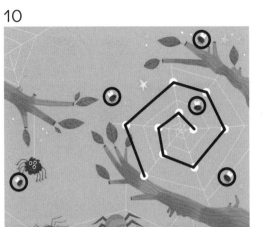

13

17

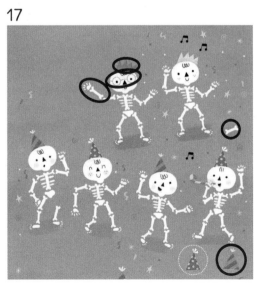

22

24

25

Answers

26

28

30

33

35

38

41

42

44

d	n	e	o	w	l
x	b	o	p	y	e
g	s	q	r	n	h
z	r	t	v	i	c
u	b	a	t	m	a
f	s	k	w	j	t

bat

owl

cat

46